BODMIN COMMUNITY COLLEGE

RESOURCES

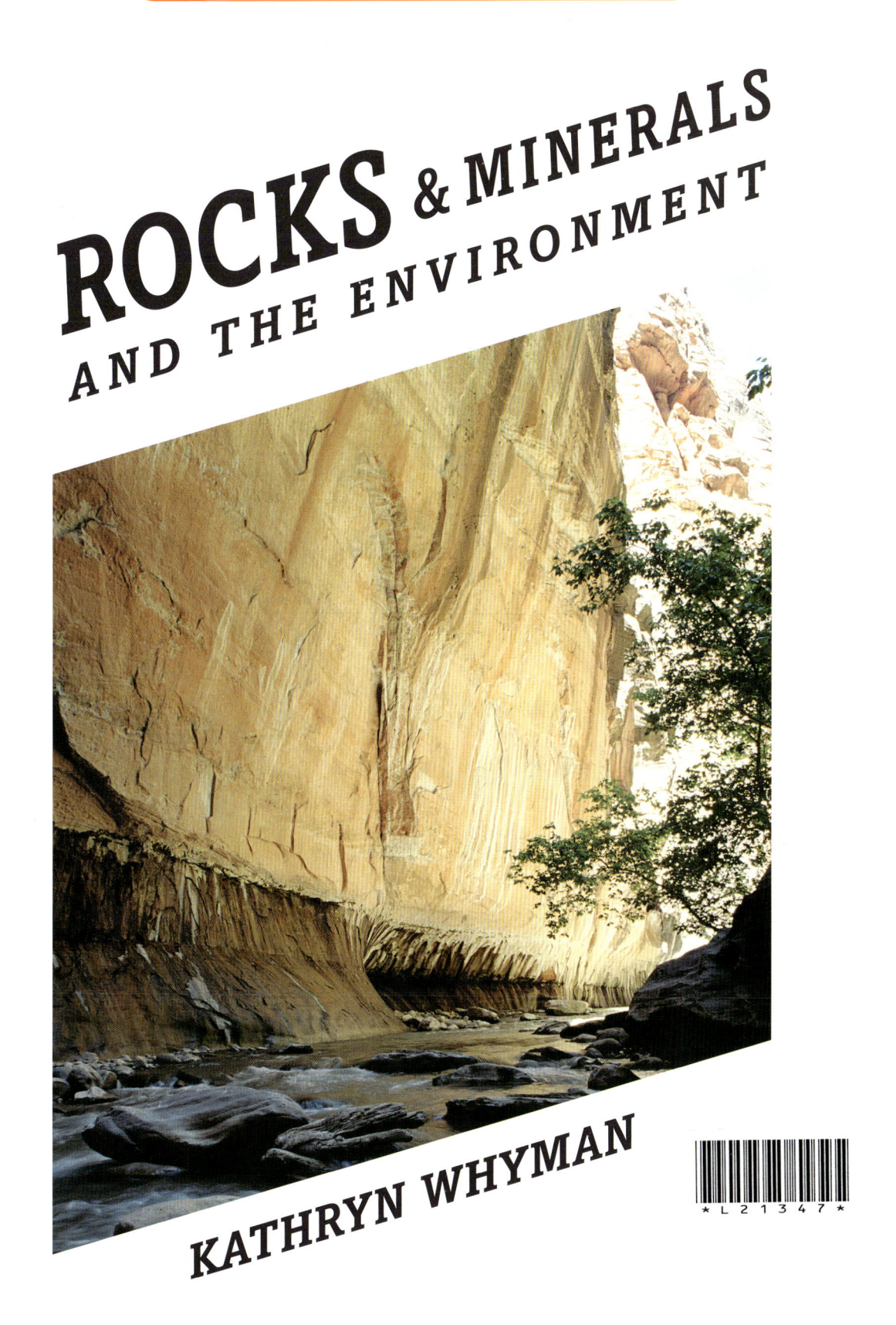

ROCKS & MINERALS
AND THE ENVIRONMENT

KATHRYN WHYMAN

Franklin Watts
London • Sydney

© Archon Press 2003

Produced by
Archon Press Ltd
28 Percy Street
London W1T 2BZ

New edition first published in
Great Britain in 2003 by
Franklin Watts
96 Leonard Street
London EC2A 4XD

Original edition published as
Resources Today – Rocks and Minerals

ISBN 0–7496–4973–9

A CIP record for this book is available from the British Library.

Printed in UAE
All rights reserved

Editor:
Harriet Brown

Designer:
Pete Bennett – PBD

Illustrator:
Louise Nevett

Picture Researcher:
Brian Hunter Smart

Photocredits Abbreviations: l-left, r-right, b-bottom, t-top, c-centre, m-middle. Front cover main, 20tr — Ingram Publishing. front cover mt, 11t — US Bureau of Land Management. front cover mb, 4tl, 6tl, 8tl, 9b, 10tl, 12tl, 14tl, 15, 16 both, 18tl, 20tl, 21 all, 22 both, 24tl, 26 all, 26-27, 27tl, 28tl, 30t, 31t, 32t — Corbis. 1, 2-3 — Photodisc. 4tr, 6tr, 8tr, 8b, 18b, 27mr — Digital Stock. 4bl — Bruce Coleman. 4b, 28bl — Corbis Royalty Free. 5t, 12b — NOAA. 7tr — Slovenian Embassy, London. 9t — Hutchison Library. 10tr, 23b — USDA. 12tr — U.S. Navy photo by Brian Nokell. 13 — Photosource. 14tr — Zefa. 14b, 17, 24tr, 27bl — Corel. 18tr — Select Pictures. 23, 25 both — Science Photo Library. 28tr — Flat Earth

CONTENTS

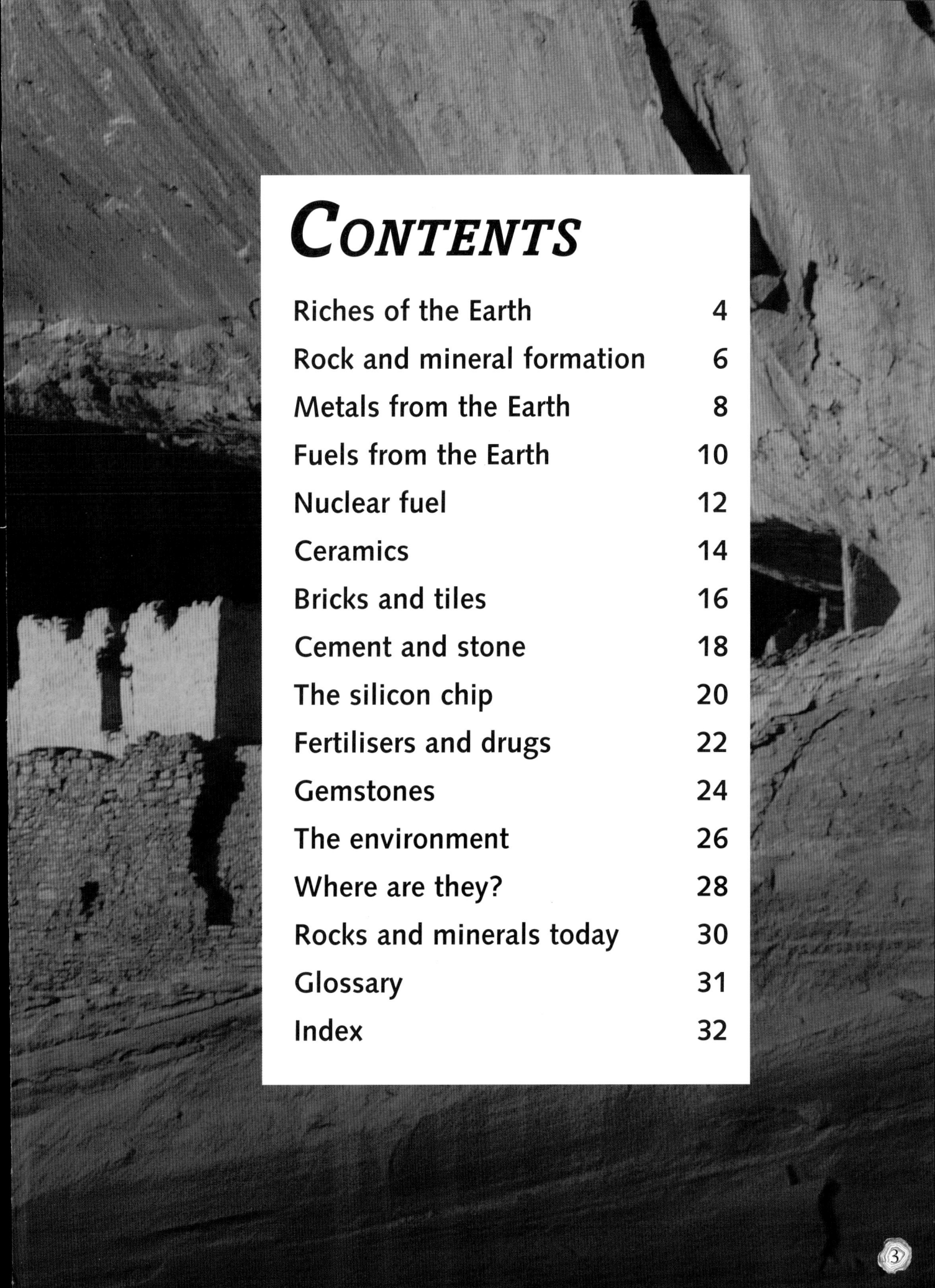

Riches of the Earth	4
Rock and mineral formation	6
Metals from the Earth	8
Fuels from the Earth	10
Nuclear fuel	12
Ceramics	14
Bricks and tiles	16
Cement and stone	18
The silicon chip	20
Fertilisers and drugs	22
Gemstones	24
The environment	26
Where are they?	28
Rocks and minerals today	30
Glossary	31
Index	32

RICHES OF THE EARTH

The Earth is a rich resource. Rocks and minerals, the raw materials of the Earth, play an important part in our lives. Buildings, fertilisers, drugs and fuels are all made from rocks and minerals – sometimes at the expense of the environment. Rocks and minerals are our oldest resource. People were making and using stone axes two million years ago. New uses are still being found for rocks and minerals. For example, today's computers would not work without silicon chips made from the mineral silica.

A limestone cave with stalagtites growing downwards

Lime is used to improve soil (inset).

A large, underwater rock formation

What are rocks and minerals?
Rocks are all the solid material of the Earth. Limestone and granite are common rocks. All rocks are made of chemical substances called minerals. Some rock types contain just one mineral. Limestone is the mineral calcium carbonate. Other rocks contain two or more different minerals. Granite is a mixture of two minerals – quartz and feldspar. Fossil fuels contain many minerals. Some minerals, for example uranium, are the source of nuclear power.

Environmental concerns
The extraction and use of rocks and minerals can destroy large areas of natural habitat and can create huge amounts of waste. The burning of fossil fuels pollutes the atmosphere and the disposal of nuclear waste is currently unsatisfactory.

ROCK AND MINERAL FORMATION

The Earth's crust is made up of about 3,000 minerals. They are found in three types of rock – igneous, sedimentary and metamorphic – or as mineral deposits. Many rocks and minerals are mined because they are useful. Rocks such as granite may be found in large deposits near the surface. Salt, a mineral, can be produced by evaporating sea water.

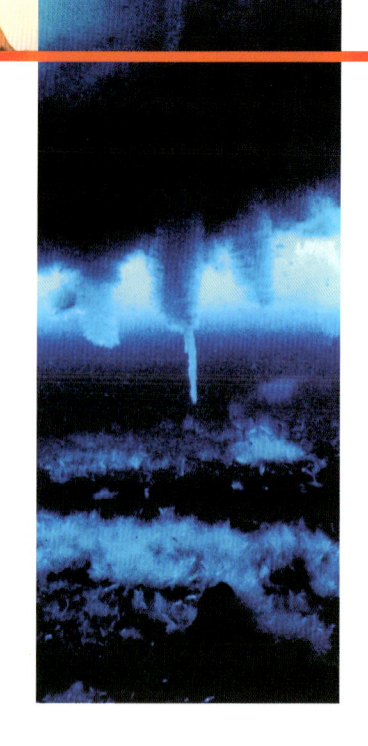

Igneous rocks
These rocks are formed when molten rock (magma) cools and becomes solid. Granite is created beneath the Earth's crust in this way (1). Sometimes magma bursts through the crust as lava and cools to form volcanic rocks like basalt (2).

Sedimentary rocks
Wind and water carry and deposit rock particles. Rivers lay down rocks like shale (3), and others like sandstone are deposited by the wind (4). Limestone is created when plant and animal skeletons build up on the beds of lakes and seas (5).

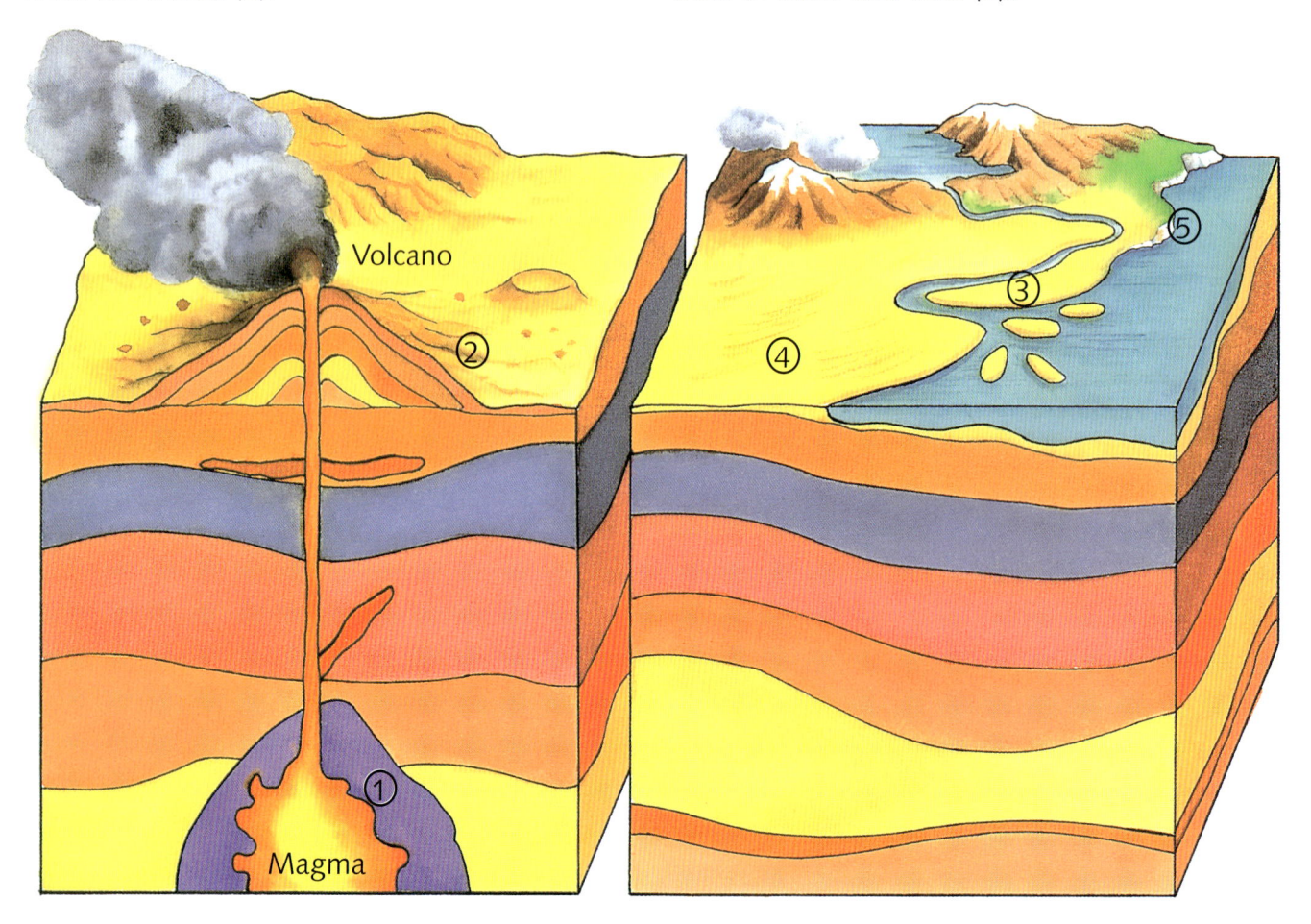

Other rocks and minerals are much harder to find. Many are only found deep beneath the Earth's surface. Diamonds are often found far underground. Most deposits of oil and gas are also deep below the surface – and some are covered by ocean water or polar ice. It is usually only worth mining rocks and minerals like these when they are found in large quantities in one place. Many tests and surveys are carried out before the exact location for a mine is chosen.

Salt is produced by evaporating sea water.

Metamorphic rocks
Rocks that are buried deep down may be changed into metamorphic rocks like slate by the pressure and heat (6). Magma may also heat the crust next to it so much that new rocks like marble are created (7).

Mineral deposits
Many valuable minerals are deposited by water. Some, like iron minerals, come from water left over when magma cools (8). Others, such as copper minerals, are formed by trapped sea water that is warmed up (9).

Metals from the Earth

Metals are a very important group of minerals. They are used in so many ways that it is hard to imagine life without them. Iron is used to make steel for building, copper makes electric wires, and aluminium is used to make all sorts of things from metal foil to aeroplanes.

A few metals are found in their pure form. More often, metals occur as part of a mineral which contains other substances. If this mixture is worth mining, it's called an ore. Bauxite is a mineral rich in aluminium. Ores like bauxite are mined and the metals are separated from them.

Aeroplanes are made from lightweight aluminium.

A steel ingot emerging from a furnace

Many metals, such as steel and aluminium, are used in car manufacture.

FUELS FROM THE EARTH

We need energy to run our machines and to heat and light our homes, offices and factories. Much of this energy is supplied by the minerals coal, oil and gas. These fossil fuels formed from dead plants and animals which lived millions of years ago. Fossil fuels release energy when they burn. The energy may be used directly, as it is in a car engine. Or it may be used to generate electricity. Fossil fuels are also important raw materials. They are converted into many substances, from make-up to plastics.

The supply of fossil fuels will not last forever. It is important that we find alternative sources of energy which will not run out, such as wind or wave power.

Coal, oil and gas formation

This diagram shows how fossil fuels were formed millions of years ago. At this time, some parts of the Earth were covered with swamps, trees and ferns. Tiny plants and animals lived in the seas. When the forest plants died they were covered by layers of mud and sand (1). When the plants and animals in the sea died, their bodies sank to the sea bed (2). Here they became trapped in layers of mud, which gradually formed rock. Buried deep underground, the tree and fern remains slowly turned into coal. The plants and animals in the mudrock got hot and formed oil and natural gas which was trapped within other rock structures (3). Now we dig mines to get the coal out of the ground and drill down to extract oil and gas (4).

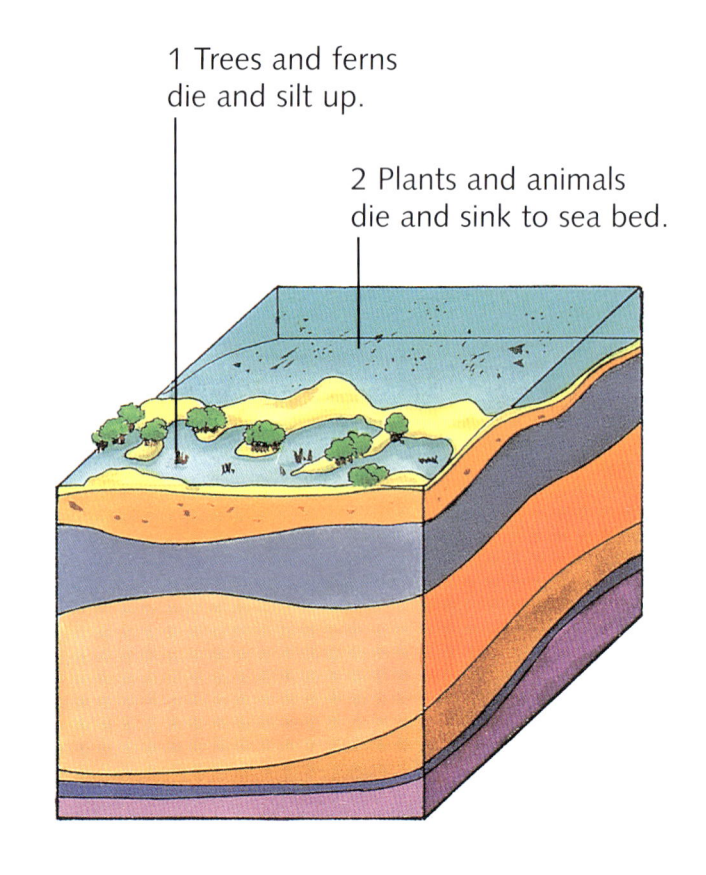

1 Trees and ferns die and silt up.

2 Plants and animals die and sink to sea bed.

Oil is transported hundreds of miles from where it is extracted to where it is used.

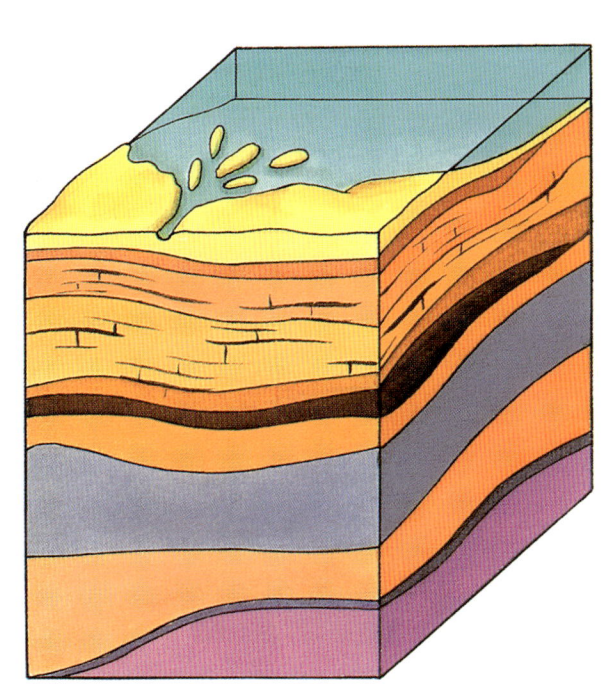

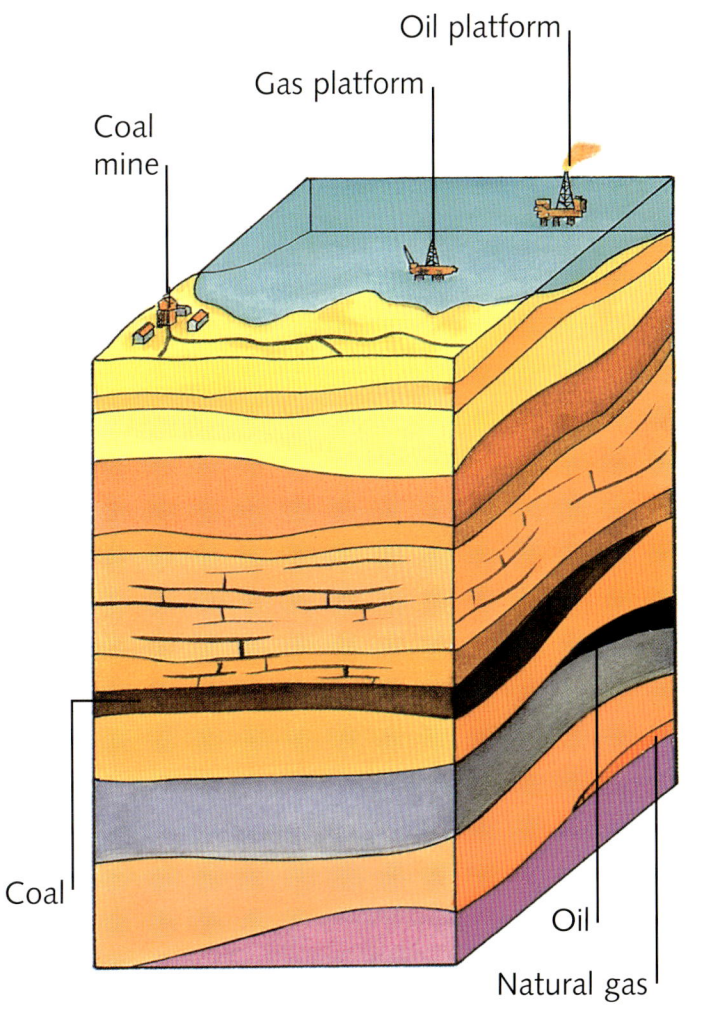

3 Fossil fuels form as plant and animal remains are buried by layers of rock.

Coal mine

Gas platform

Oil platform

Coal

Oil

Natural gas

Nuclear fuel

An alternative to fossil fuels is nuclear fuel. The metal uranium gives out energy called radioactivity. Uranium is found as an ore and is mined. The ore is ground into a powder and dissolved in chemicals to obtain the pure metal. Specially treated uranium undergoes reactions in which its atoms split to produce vast amounts of energy. This energy is then used to generate electricity.

Nuclear radiation can be dangerous. In 1986, in the former USSR, the Chernobyl nuclear power station exploded. The radioactivity that leaked out contributed to the deaths of thousands of people. Nuclear power is also used to make dangerous weapons.

A nuclear power station in the United States

nucleus

neutron

Energy is released

Nuclear fission

It is the process of nuclear fission, inside nuclear reactors, which creates the energy supplied by nuclear power. A neutron hits a uranium nucleus. This splits the nucleus, releasing more neutrons and a lot of energy.

Inside a nuclear power plant – uranium must be handled with extreme caution.

Ceramics

Many rocks and minerals can be baked to make materials called ceramics. Some ceramics will be familiar to you – bricks are ceramics, and so are most bowls, plates and mugs. Ceramics have some very useful properties. They are usually hard and they do not rot or rust. They do not let heat or electricity flow through them easily – they are good insulators.

Scientists have discovered that some ceramics, called superconductors, conduct electricity at low temperatures without heating up or expanding. Superconductors are used in electric circuits and engine parts.

Bowls and plates are ceramics.

The underneath surfaces of space shuttles are covered in ceramic tiles. These protect the shuttle from the intense heat it experiences when it re-enters the Earth's atmosphere.

The launch of the space shuttle Atlantis

BRICKS AND TILES

Unless it is made of wood, your home is probably built from rocks and minerals. Perhaps it is made of bricks. Bricks make excellent building materials – they are hardly affected by the weather and they don't burn. Bricks are made from clay, a soft rock that comes in many forms. Clay is found and mined in many countries in the world. It is then fired (baked) in a kiln.

Bricks come in different colours and qualities. This depends on the chemicals in the clay. Bricks can also be made from a mixture of lime and sand. These bricks are normally white or grey. Roof tiles are made in a similar way to bricks.

Making bricks

First the clay or shale (rock made from clay) is crushed. This happens at least twice. Oversize particles are screened out and put back into the crushers. When the particles are fine enough, they are fed into a container and mixed with water. Wet clay is then pushed through an extruder, which moulds the clay into a ribbon. Hollows may be pushed into the top of each brick before the bricks are cut and separated. The bricks are dried and fired in a kiln.

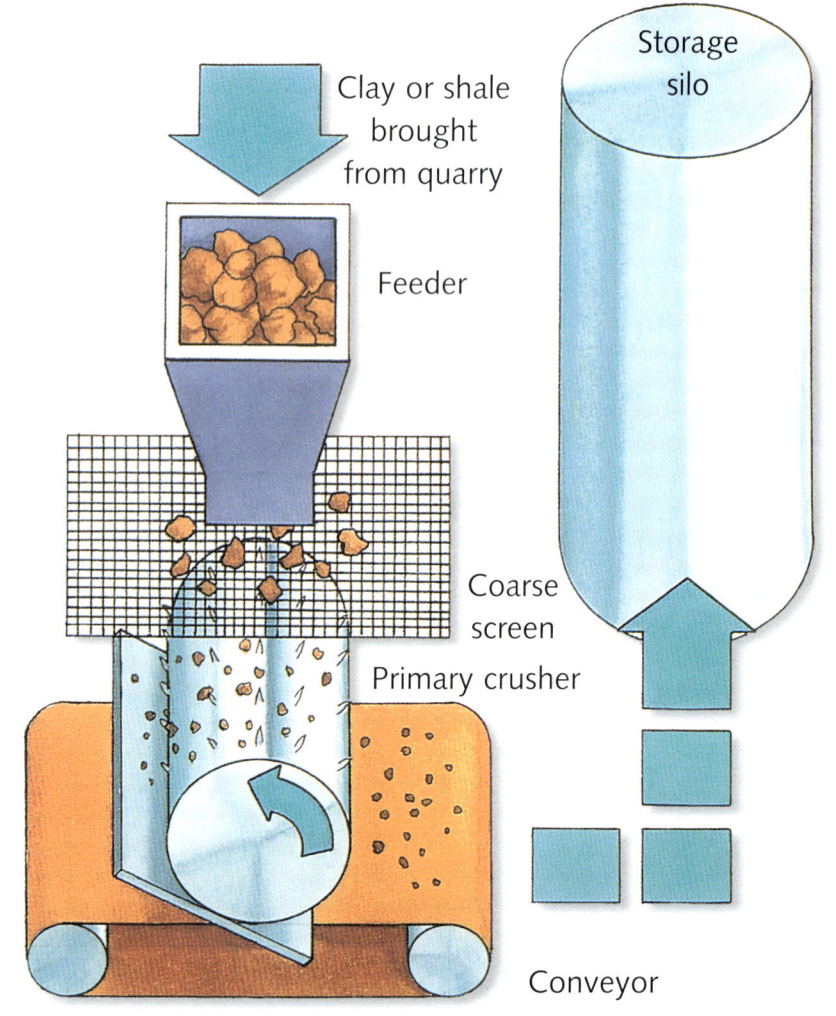

Clay or shale brought from quarry

Feeder

Coarse screen

Primary crusher

Storage silo

Conveyor

Bricks being made by hand

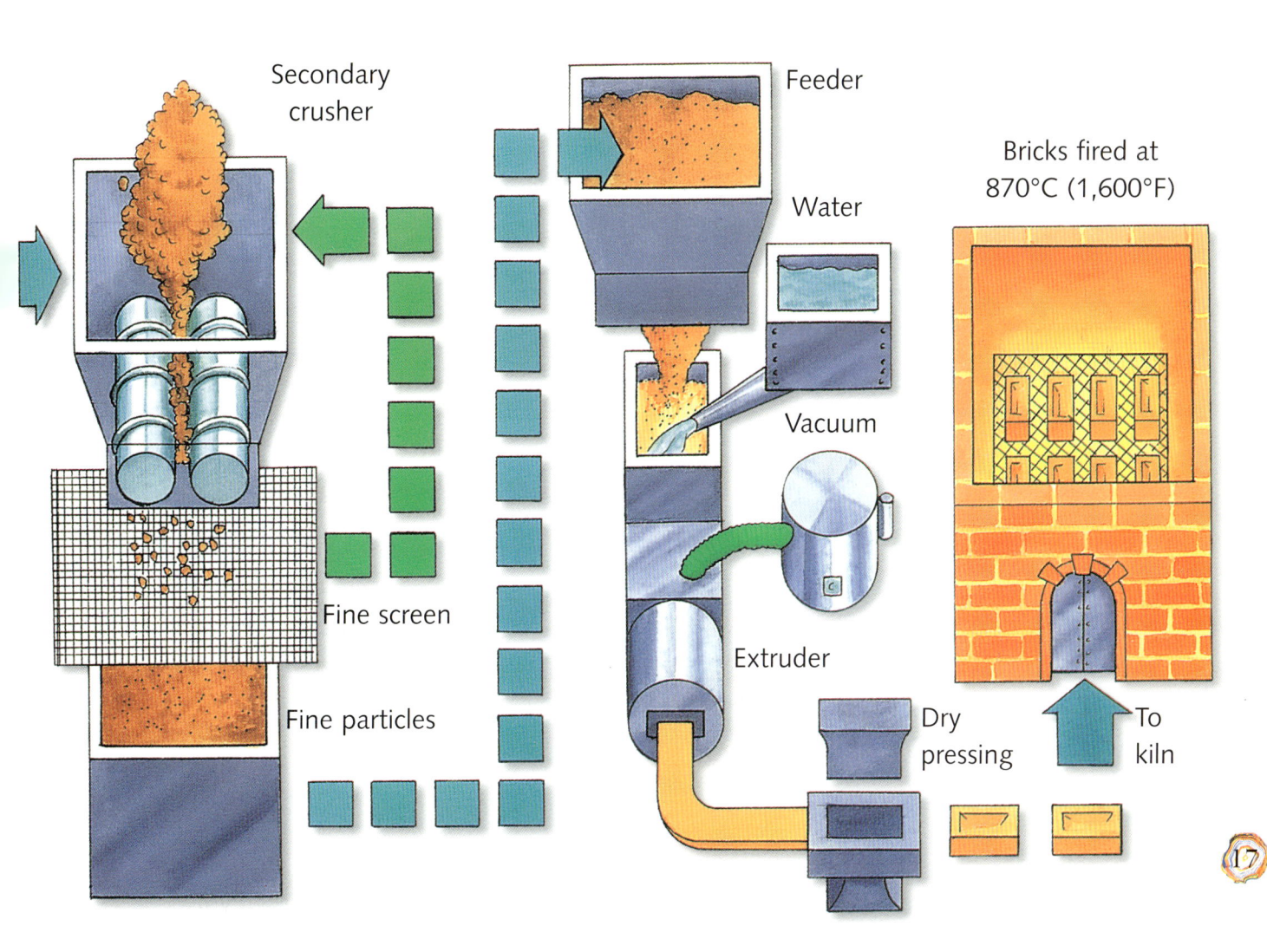

Secondary crusher

Feeder

Water

Bricks fired at 870°C (1,600°F)

Vacuum

Fine screen

Extruder

Fine particles

Dry pressing

To kiln

Cement and Stone

Some rocks can simply be cut into blocks for building. Sandstone, granite and limestone are all building stones. Slate is a type of clay which forms in sheets. It can be cut into flat blocks for roofs or paving stones. Marble, a rock formed from limestone, is smooth and colourful. It is used for sculpture and decoration because of its attractive appearance.

Limestone has another important use in building – it is the main constituent of cement. Cement is used to make mortar, which holds bricks together, and concrete. Concrete is our most important building material – bridges, buildings, dams and roads are all made with it.

Many modern bridges are made using concrete.

Manufacturing cement

Cement is made from shale, limestone and other rocks and minerals. These raw materials are ground into fine particles and blended in the correct proportions. The mixture is then fired in a hot kiln. This produces brittle lumps called clinker. Once the clinker has cooled it is ground to make cement. Concrete is made by mixing cement with water, sand and gravel.

Blending silos

Dust collector

Kiln feeder

Heat

Materials fired in rotary kiln to produce clinker

Grinder

Clinker grinder

Raw materials brought from quarries

Dryer

Clinker cooler

Crusher

Cement stored in silos

Raw materials (limestone, shale, shells, clay, iron ore slag and silica)

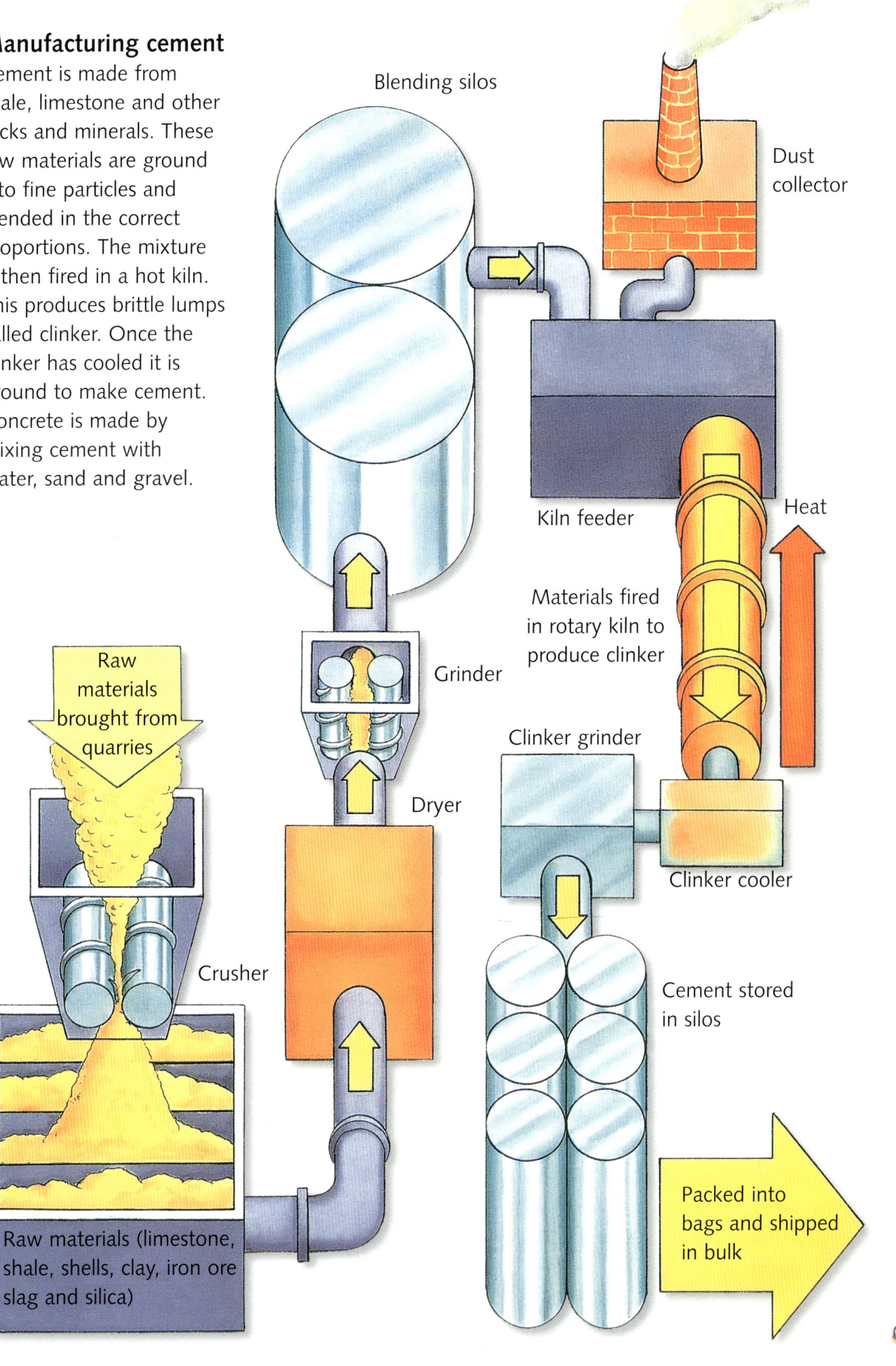

Packed into bags and shipped in bulk

THE SILICON CHIP

Silica, or silicon dioxide, is one of the most common materials in the Earth's crust – sand is full of it. Silica is the raw material used to produce silicon chips.

A chip is a tiny piece of silicon smaller than your fingernail. The tiny chip is packed with millions of transistors which can process vast amounts of information. The smaller the components of a computer chip are, the faster the information can be processed by a computer. Today, computer companies are looking for ways of shaping smaller and smaller circuits onto silicon chips.

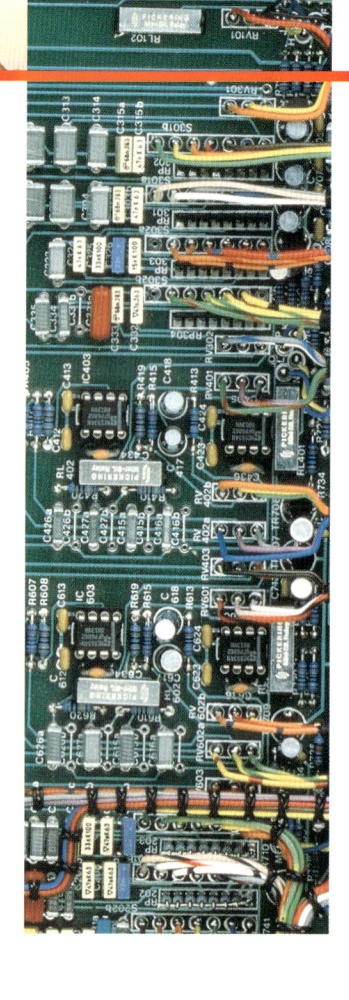

1 Crystals of quartz

2 Pure silicon rod

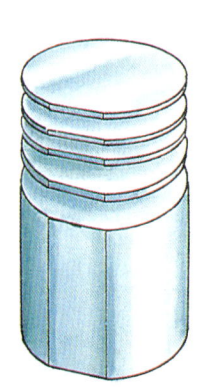

3 More impurities removed by zone refining

4 Thin wafers sliced from rod

Heating wires

Preparing silicon for chips

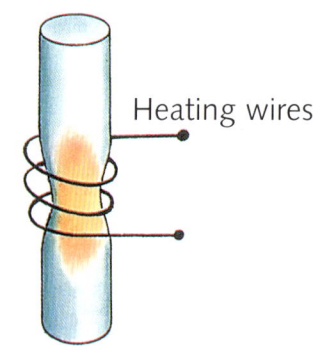

Because the circuits on a chip are so small, the silicon used to make it must be very pure. First silicon dioxide, found in sand and quartz rocks (1), is changed into the form of a single crystal where all the particles of silicon are arranged in orderly rows. This is done using a tiny crystal – called a seed crystal – to grow a rod of pure silicon (2). More impurities are pushed out by melting and cooling the rod in the process called zone refining (3). It is then sliced into thin wafers, each about 10 cm in diameter (4). One wafer will make many chips.

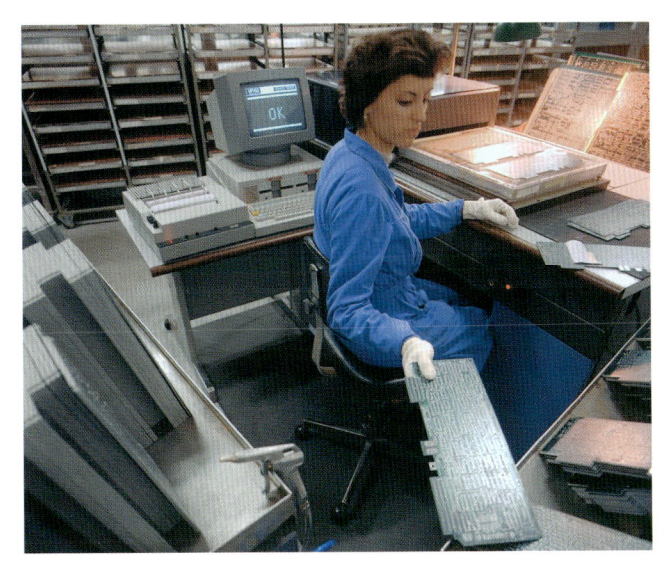

Ultra-violet light is shined through a mask onto a silicon wafer to make the tiny circuits.

Lenses are used to focus the ultra-violet light onto the silicon wafers.

FERTILISERS AND DRUGS

Living things need minerals to keep healthy. Humans get most of the minerals they need from food. For example, milk contains calcium needed for strong teeth and bones.

Many drugs contain minerals such as mercury and iodine. Chemicals from crude oil are used to make a wide range of drugs.

Fertilisers, which are special mixtures of minerals, are used to help plants grow. The most important minerals in fertilisers are nitrates, phosphates and potassium salts. Large quantities of fertilisers are made from these minerals. Farmers then add them to the soil.

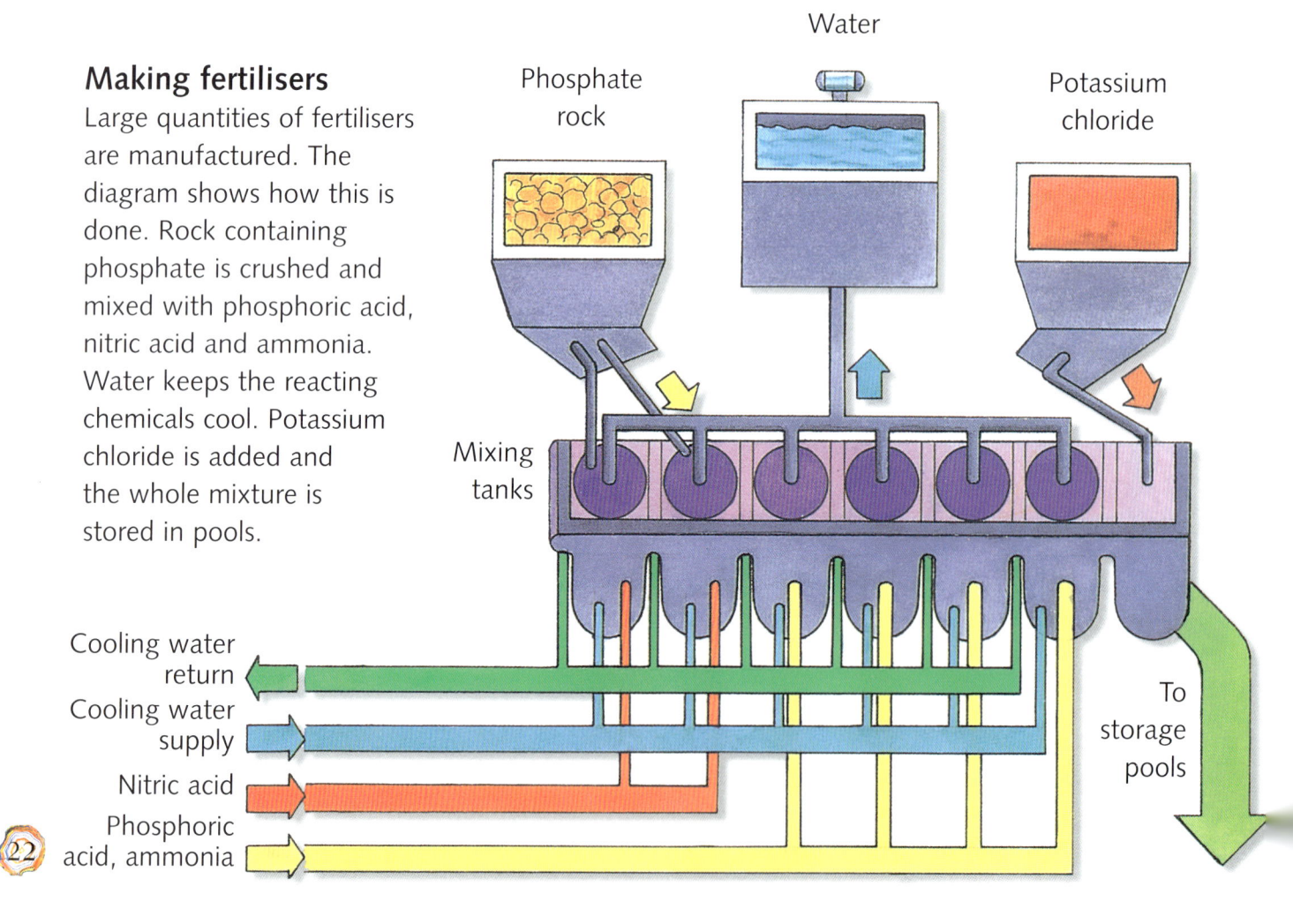

Making fertilisers

Large quantities of fertilisers are manufactured. The diagram shows how this is done. Rock containing phosphate is crushed and mixed with phosphoric acid, nitric acid and ammonia. Water keeps the reacting chemicals cool. Potassium chloride is added and the whole mixture is stored in pools.

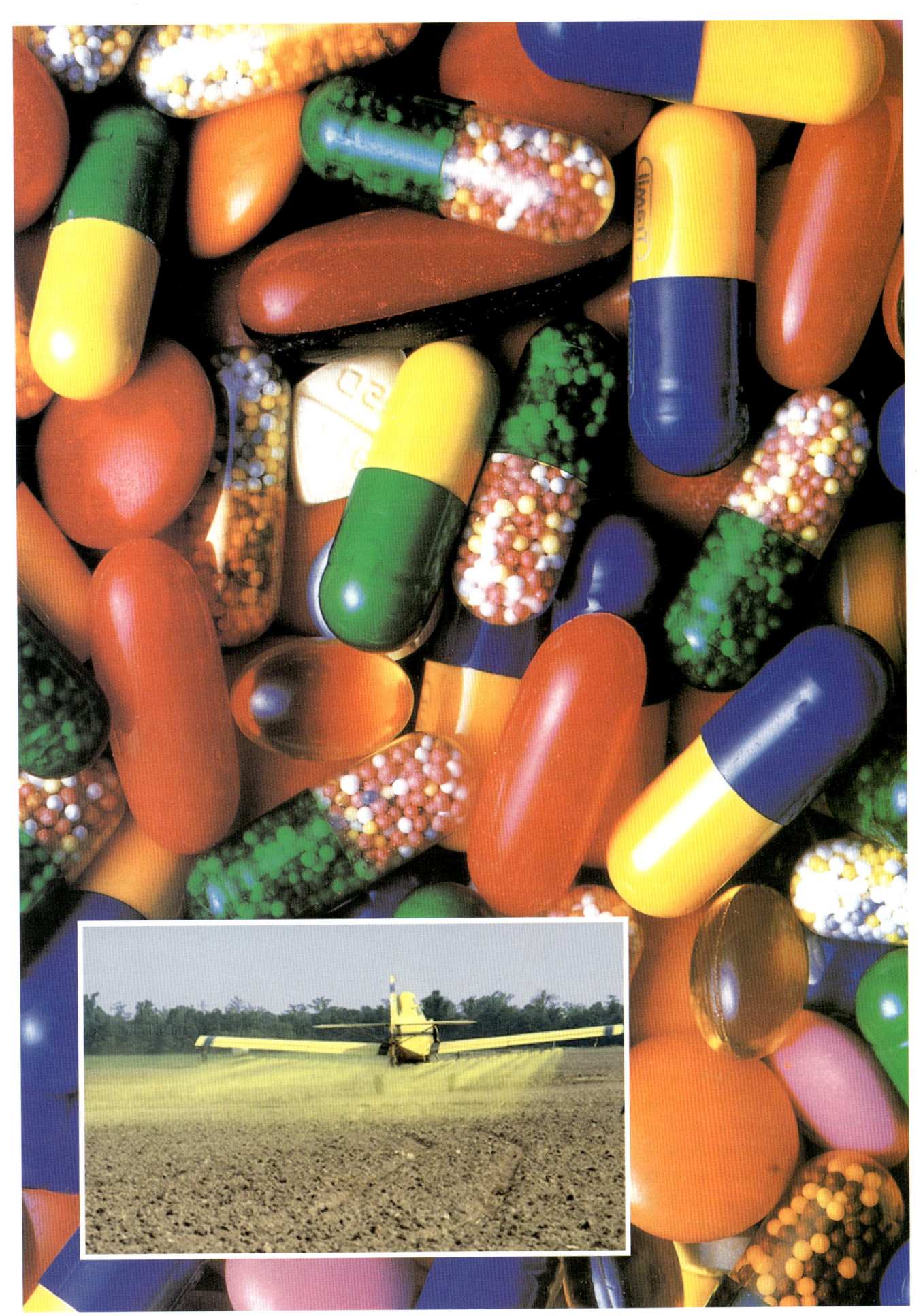

Many drugs are made with chemicals from oil. Fertilisers are sprayed on crops (inset).

Gemstones

Some minerals form beautiful crystals. These crystals are called gems. Gems have to be dug out of the Earth. Diamonds come from very big, deep mines. Other gems, like opal, topaz and emerald, are mined closer to the surface. Gems are used to make jewellery, but also have important uses in industry.

Diamond is the hardest material known. Small or poorly coloured diamonds, called industrial diamonds, are used to make saws which can cut through steel. Diamond powder and grit is also made artificially for this purpose. Quartz crystal vibrates regularly when a small electric current is applied to it. It is used in clocks and watches.

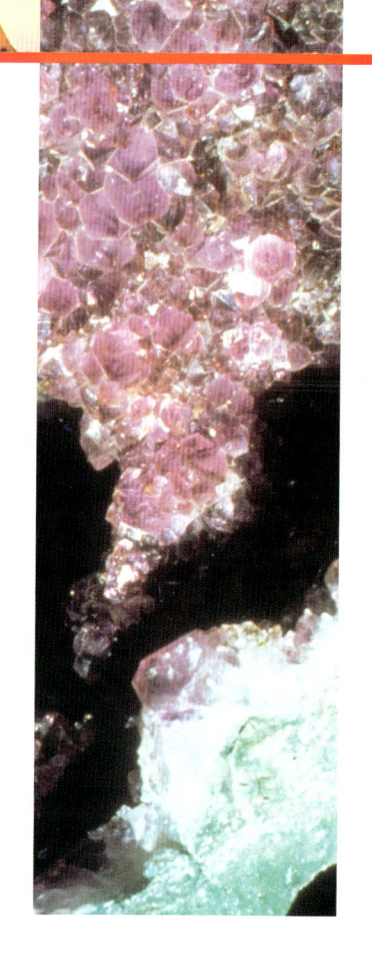

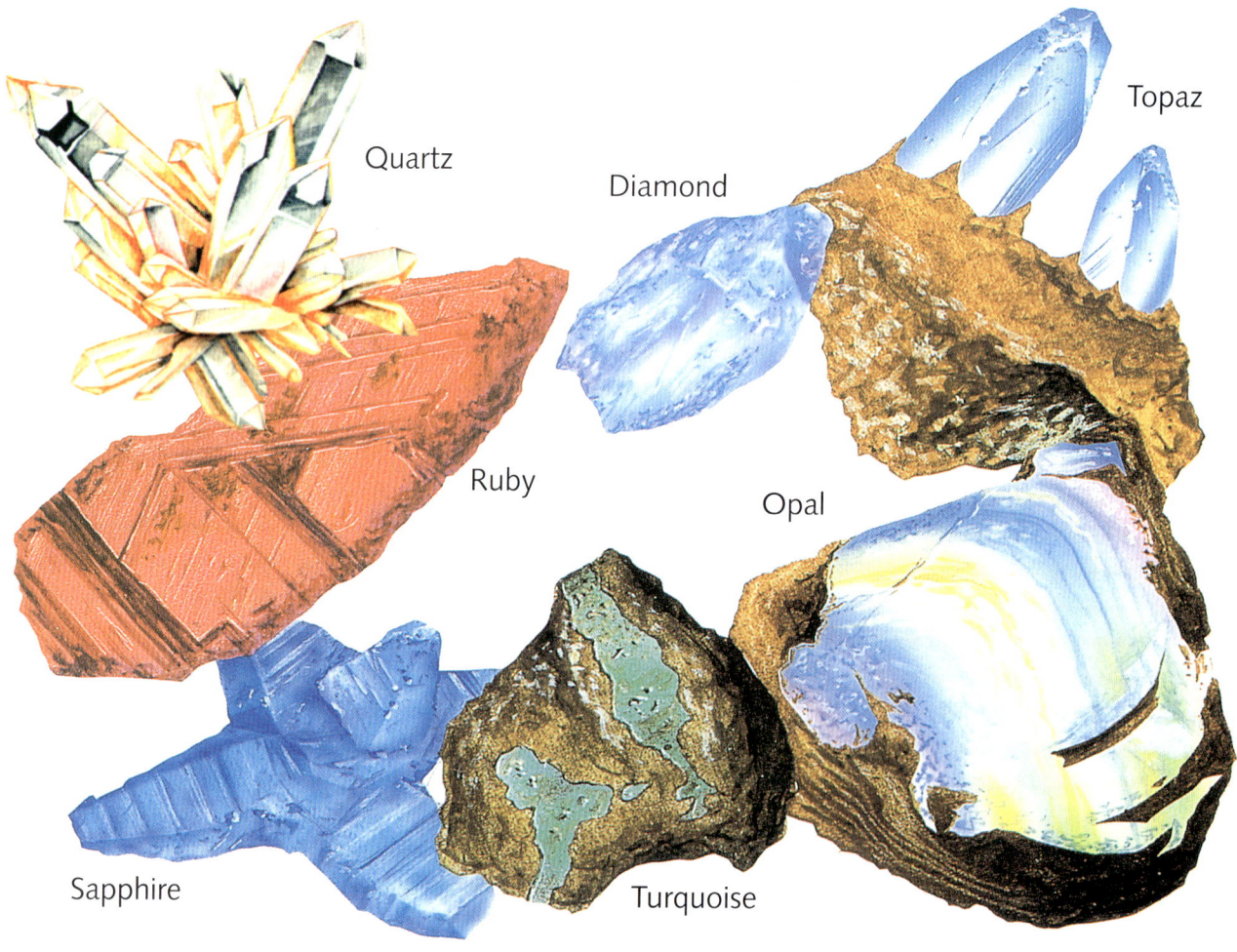

Quartz

Diamond

Topaz

Ruby

Opal

Sapphire

Turquoise

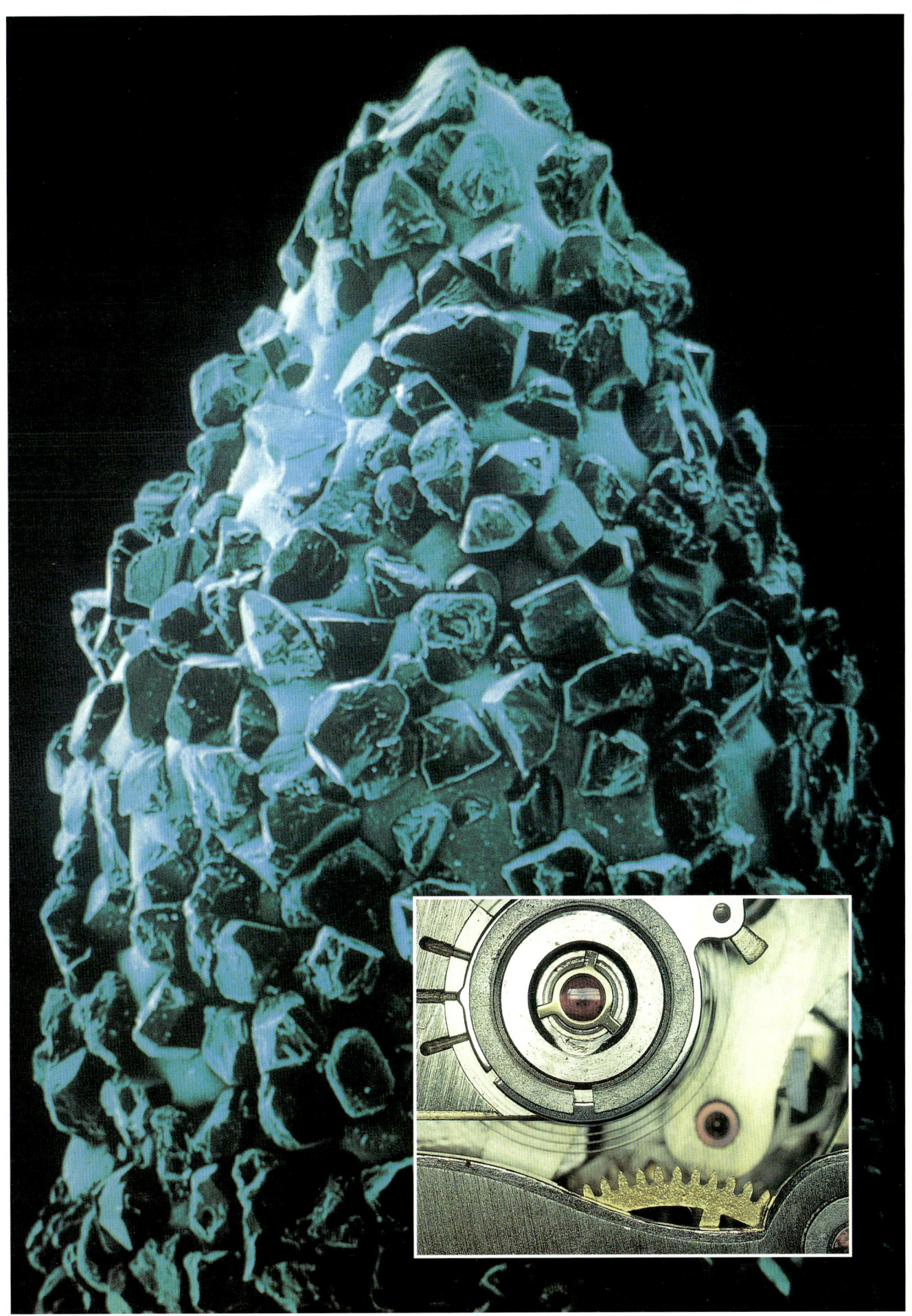

This dentist's drill has a surface of diamond grit. Quartz crystal is used in clocks and watches (inset).

THE ENVIRONMENT

Rocks and minerals are widely used in our daily activities. We depend on rocks and minerals for building materials, fuel, fertilisers, drugs and even computers. However, extracting and using some of these substances can have a damaging effect on the environment in which we live. It can scar the landscape, pollute the planet and harm wildlife.

▼ Alternative sources
Rocks and minerals will not last forever, particularly fossil fuels. However, there are places we could look for new mineral sources. The deep sea bed and outer space are largely undiscovered. Perhaps one day humans will be mining for rocks in these faraway places.

▲ Energy
Machines used in quarries and mines to extract rocks and minerals from the Earth consume lots of energy. Energy is also needed to make fertilisers, crush and cut rocks, find gemstones and make cement and concrete. Coal, oil and gas provide this energy and they are in danger of running out before other rocks and minerals do. Different energy sources are being researched by scientists.

◀ **Recycling**
It is important to recycle as many raw materials as we can. Glass and ceramics can be recycled. Old bricks can be cleaned and then re-used, or crushed and used as part of a building's foundations. Try to conserve energy by closing windows and doors to stop heat from escaping and by switching off lights when they're not in use.

▼ **Tourism and pollution**
Rock formations can be damaged by people touching them and walking on them. Acid rain, caused by the burning of fossil fuels, can erode rocks such as The Giant's Causeway in Northern Ireland. This can be very damaging over a period of time.

▲ **Wildlife**
Mining can destroy wide areas of natural habitat. To extract rocks and minerals from the Earth, vegetation and soil must first be removed. This can lead to erosion of the land and damage to the local wildlife, including rare plant species, endangered mammals, reptiles, birds, amphibians and insects. Roads also supply mines and these too can have a damaging effect on the natural habitat.

Where are they?

Chemical and fertiliser minerals include sulphur, rock salt, borax and phosphate rock. The largest deposits of these are in Europe, Africa and the Americas. Some 90 per cent of the world's sulphur comes from Louisiana and Texas in the United States. Diamonds, the most important gemstone, are mined in the Democratic Republic of Congo, South Africa and the former USSR.

More iron is produced than any other metal. Every year, 900 million tonnes of iron ore are mined. The main deposits are in the former USSR. The light metal aluminium is mined in the United States, the former USSR, Japan and Australia. Uranium is a rare metal which is mined in the United States, Australia and the Democratic Republic of Congo.

Other industrial minerals include asbestos, china clay, mica and talc. The biggest deposits are in the United States, Europe and the former USSR.

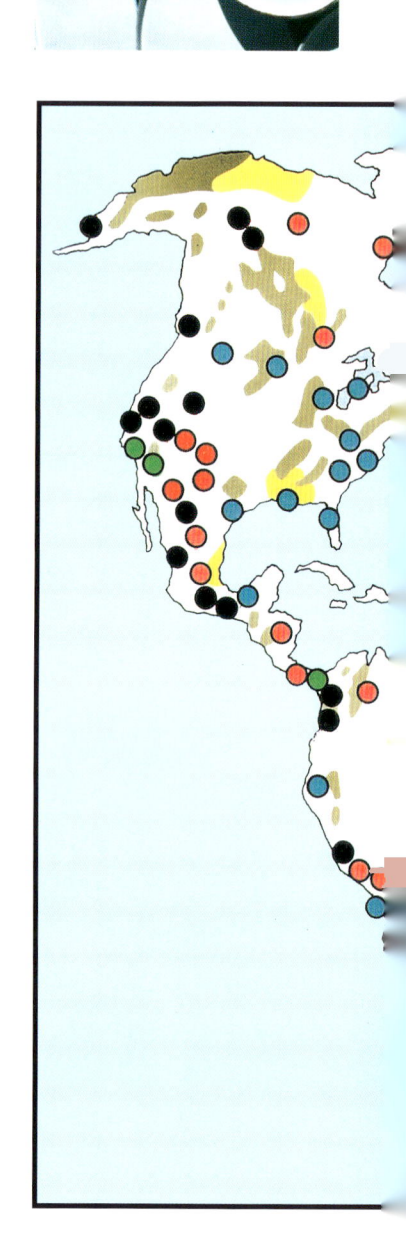

The largest deposits of gold are in South Africa.

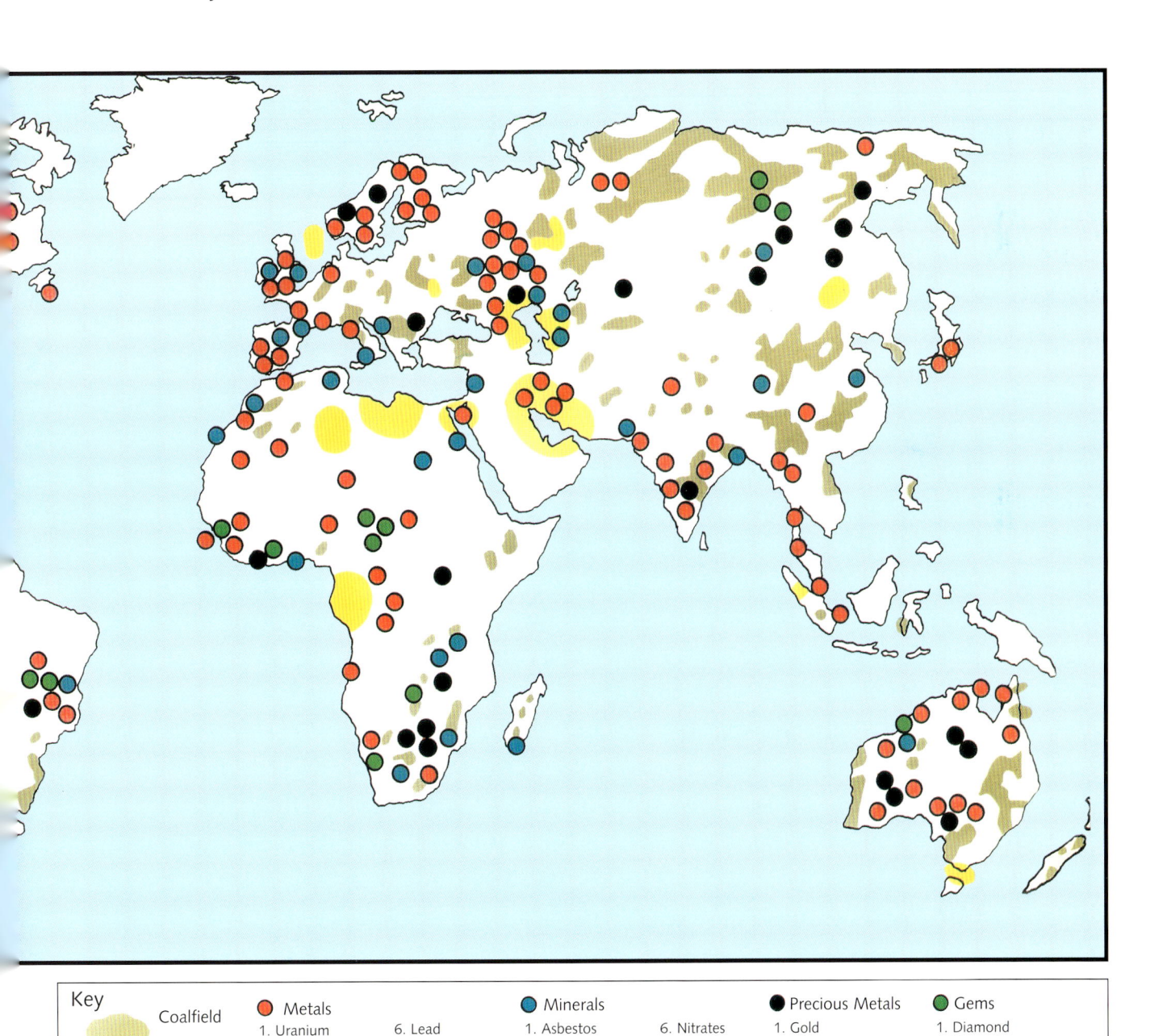

Fossil fuels

Every day we use over 55 million barrels of oil. More than half the known reserves of oil are in the Middle East. Saudi Arabia exports more oil than any other country.

Coal is found on every continent. The United States and the former USSR have the largest reserves. Hard coals are a lot older than soft coals and provide more energy by weight. Coal reserves will last much longer than reserves of oil and gas. So demand for coal is likely to increase in the future.

Key					
Coalfield	🔴 Metals		🔵 Minerals	⚫ Precious Metals	🟢 Gems
	1. Uranium	6. Lead	1. Asbestos 6. Nitrates	1. Gold	1. Diamond
	2. Iron	7. Mercury	2. Clay 7. Phosphate	2. Silver	2. Turquoise
Oilfield	3. Manganese	8. Tin	3. Mica 8. Potash	3. Platinum	3. Emerald
	4. Nickel	9. Zinc	4. Talc 9. Rock salt		
	5. Copper	10. Aluminium	5. Borax 10. Sulphur		

ROCKS AND MINERALS TODAY

Rocks and minerals are found all over the world. We use them in our everyday lives without even realising it. Here is a list of some of the more unusual rocks and minerals and their uses.

Product	How it is extracted	What it is used for
SALT	Solution mining is used to extract deposits underground. Sea water may be evaporated.	Salt is added to food to preserve it or to enhance taste. It consists of sodium and chlorine.
QUARTZ	Quartz may be mined from granite rocks or extracted from sand or gravel.	It is used in watches and optical instruments. It is a source of silica, which is used to make silicon chips.
GRAPHITE	Graphite is mined from rocks such as gneiss and schist.	It is used as 'lead' in pencils, as a lubricant, in paint and to make parts for electric motors.
BORAX	Borax is obtained from the beds of dry salt lakes or by evaporating sea water.	It is used in bleaches, soaps and detergents. It is also added to ceramics and fertilisers.
PHOSPHATE	Phosphate comes from phosphate rock, which is mined. Sea bird droppings also contain it.	It is used in match heads and in some medicines. But its main use is in fertilisers.
TITANIUM	Minerals containing it are mined and it is extracted in a protected atmosphere.	Titanium is used to make pigment for paints. It is a light, strong metal used in jet engines.
PLATINUM	Platinum is extracted from some metal ores. It must be smelted and refined.	It is used to make jewellery and wires. It is used in dentistry, in jet engines and to coat missile nose cones.
SULPHUR	Sulphur is mined by being melted with hot steam. It is also extracted from some metal ores.	Its main use is the manufacture of sulphuric acid for industrial uses such as making fertiliser.
FLUORITE	Fluorite is found in mines in its pure, crystal form. Other minerals such as quartz can be found attached to it.	It is quite a soft gem and is therefore mainly used to make jewellery such as earrings.

GLOSSARY

Cement
Cement is a substance used to make mortar and concrete. It is made from shale, limestone and other rocks and minerals.

Concrete
A strong building material. Concrete is a mixture of sand, cement, stone and water which sets hard. It sets by a chemical reaction rather than just by drying out.

Crystal
A substance whose particles are in a neat, orderly pattern. Most minerals occur naturally in the form of crystals.

Erosion
The wearing down and breaking up of rocks by natural forces such as the wind, rain, ice, snow and running water.

Fertiliser
A substance containing chemicals needed for healthy plant growth. Farmers spray fertiliser on crops to help them grow. The main minerals used in fertilisers are nitrates, phosphates and potassium salts.

Fossil fuels
Substances made from dead and decayed living things which produce energy when they are burned. Coal, oil and natural gas are fossil fuels.

Igneous rocks
Rocks formed when molten rock cools and becomes solid. Granite is created in this way.

Kiln
A type of oven. Ceramics are baked (fired) in kilns.

Metamorphic rocks
Rocks deep under the Earth that have been heated or squashed to create new rocks. Marble is created in this way.

Mineral
Chemical substances which are found in the Earth's crust. Minerals are the basic natural substances that make up rocks.

Mortar
A paste made of a mixture of sand, cement and water which sets hard when it dries. Mortar is used to hold bricks together in building.

Ore
A mineral which is worth mining because it contains a valuable substance such as a metal. Iron is found as an ore mineral.

Radioactivity
A form of energy that is given out by some materials. Uranium is a radioactive metal and is used to create nuclear power. Radioactive metals are also used to make nuclear weapons.

Sedimentary rocks
Rocks that are formed as a result of being deposited by the wind or water. Sandstone is deposited by the wind.

Smelting
A process used to separate metals in an ore. Platinum is extracted in this way.

Superconductor
A substance that will conduct electricity without heating up or expanding. Certain ceramics are superconductors.

Wafer
A thin slice of pure silicon. One wafer will make many silicon chips.

INDEX

A
aluminium 8, 9, 28
atmosphere 5, 30

B
basalt 6
bauxite 8
bricks 14, 16, 17, 18, 27, 31
bridges 18
buildings 4, 8, 18, 26, 27, 31

C
calcium 5, 22
cement 18, 19, 26, 31
ceramics 14, 27, 30, 31
clay 16, 28
coal 10, 11, 26, 28, 29, 31
computer 4, 20, 26
concrete 18, 19, 26, 31
copper 7, 8
crystals 20, 24, 26, 30, 31

D
diamond 7, 24, 25, 28
drugs 4, 22, 23, 26, 30

E
energy 10, 12, 13, 26, 27

F
feldspar 5
fertilisers 4, 22, 23, 26, 28, 29, 30, 31
food 22, 30
fossil fuels 5, 10, 11, 12, 26, 27, 28, 29, 31
fuels 4, 10, 11, 26

G
gas 7, 10, 11, 26, 28, 29, 31
gems 7, 24, 25, 26, 28, 29, 30, 31
glass 27
gold 28
granite 5, 6, 18, 30, 31
graphite 30

H
habitat 5

I
igneous rocks 6, 31
industry 4, 8, 9, 10, 14, 15, 20, 24, 28, 30, 31
iron 7, 8, 28, 31

L
lava 6
limestone 4, 5, 6, 16, 18, 19, 31

M
magma 6, 7
marble 7, 18
mercury 22
metals 7, 8, 9, 12, 28, 29, 30, 31
metamorphic rocks 6, 7, 31
mineral deposits 7, 28, 29, 30, 31
mining 6, 7, 8, 10, 11, 12, 16, 24, 26, 28, 30, 31
mortar 18, 31

N
nuclear:
 fission 13
 fuel 5, 12, 13, 31

O
oil 7, 10, 11, 22, 23, 26, 28, 29, 31
ores 8, 12, 28, 30, 31

Q
quartz 5, 20, 24, 25, 26, 30

R
radiation 12, 31
recycling 27
rocks:
 composition 5
 formation 6, 7
 types 5, 6, 7, 16, 18, 30
 uses 4, 14, 16, 18, 19, 30

S
salt 6, 30
sandstone 6, 16, 18, 19, 20, 30, 31
sedimentary rocks 6, 31
shale 6, 16, 19, 31
silica 4, 19, 20, 26
silicon chip 4, 20, 21, 31
slate 18
space shuttles 15
stalagtites 4
steel 8, 9
stones 4, 5, 6, 18, 19, 31
superconductors 14, 31

U
uranium 5, 12, 13, 28, 31

W
wildlife 27